ANDY STANLEY

IF
MONEY
TALKED

Four Things It Would Tell You

Financial Advice That Will Make Your Life Better and Make You Better at Life

Contents

FROM THE AUTHOR

People get nervous when I preach about money.

I get it. The church has a checkered reputation when it comes to money.

But do you know what's fascinating? *Money is what people want to talk to the church about all the time.* When someone comes in with a challenge or request for advice, their situation is often related to money.

We all seem to understand that faith and finances are connected. We just don't want to admit it.

So, if there's something in you that wants to stiff-arm a Bible study about money, I understand. If you think God doesn't belong in your bank account, I can appreciate that. I hope you'll stick around anyway.

You'll find out that this study isn't about God getting your money. It's not a plan for getting out of debt or avoiding bankruptcy (though I hope you do both). It's about something much deeper. In fact, you could be completely out of debt, have lots of money in the bank, have college tuition paid for, and still be in a ditch financially.

How is that possible? I'm so glad you asked.

—Andy

How to Use the Study

 1 ▶ Watch.

As a group, watch the session video. *(See page 7 for instructions.)*

 2 ▶ Discuss.

As a group, talk through the discussion questions found after the video notes in each chapter.

 3 ▶ Dig in.

On your own, complete the homework activities and the session reading before your group meets again.

LEAD A GROUP

If you are leading a group through this study, check out

ifmoneytalked.com/leader

for tips on how to lead the discussion for each session.

How to Use the Study

ON YOUR OWN

1 ▶ Watch.

Watch the session video. *(See page 7 for instructions.)*

2 ▶ Process.

Jot down your answers to the discussion questions found after the video notes in each chapter.

3 ▶ Dig in.

Complete the homework activities and reading before moving on to the next session.

FIND EXTRA SUPPORT

If you're tackling this study on your own, check out

ifmoneytalked.com/next

to connect with someone who can answer questions and cheer you on.

Where to Watch the Videos

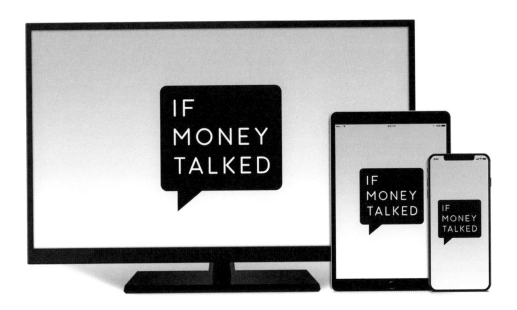

YouTube

ifmoneytalked.com/videos

anthology.study/studies/ifmoneytalked

Anthology App *(Available for your phone, tablet, and TV)*

The
Consumption
Assumption

AS A GROUP, IN SESSION 1...

(1) Watch the Session 1 video. *(14 minutes)*

(2) Discuss the questions that begin on page 12.

ON YOUR OWN, BEFORE SESSION 2...

(1) Follow the instructions on page 16 to take the Money Quiz.

(2) Read more about your quiz result and find answers to common questions beginning on page 17.

I CAN ADD MEANING TO YOUR LIFE, BUT I'M NOT THE MEANING OF LIFE.

—Money

Video Notes

Time   14 MINUTES

Scripture   LUKE 12:15

▶ What do you do with your spare money?

▶ Greed is the assumption that it's all for my consumption.

WATCH OUT! BE ON YOUR GUARD AGAINST ALL KINDS OF GREED; LIFE DOES NOT CONSIST IN AN ABUNDANCE OF POSSESSIONS.

———————————————————————— *Luke 12:15*

▶ What if you began to view money as a means—a tool—to do something meaningful with your life?

▶ No one who applies what Jesus says about money to their personal finances ever regrets it.

Ready to take the money quiz? *It's recommended that you talk through the following discussion questions with your group. Then take the quiz on your own before the next session.*

Discussion Questions

1 | How was money handled in your house when you were growing up?

2 | What was modeled about money in the past often influences the assumptions you hold about money today. Let's identify what some of those may be.

A) Individually, take a few minutes to mark how you feel about each of the following statements.

> *Note: These are not necessarily right or wrong, good or bad. The goal is simply to uncover some of the things you've come to believe about money.*

1. The details of my finances should be kept private from family and friends.

2. If I work hard, I have the right to play hard.

3. My salary and my stuff are an indication of my success.

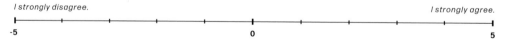

4. The more money I have in savings, the more secure I feel.

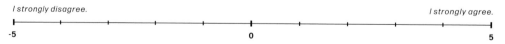

5. Some kinds of debt are okay.

6. Once I have everything I need, I should be generous with what I have left.

I strongly disagree.   *I strongly agree.*

-5   0   5

7. Financial success or failure has a lot to do with luck.

I strongly disagree.   *I strongly agree.*

-5   0   5

8. I can get myself out of a financial mess if I need to.

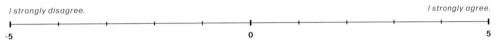

I strongly disagree.   *I strongly agree.*

-5   0   5

9. Money is meant to be spent because I can't take it with me when I die.

I strongly disagree.   *I strongly agree.*

-5   0   5

10. I know enough to confidently manage my money.

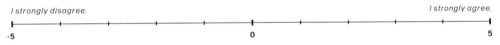

I strongly disagree.   *I strongly agree.*

-5   0   5

11. Carrying a balance due on my credit card(s) is okay.

I strongly disagree.   *I strongly agree.*

-5   0   5

12. I should not need financial assistance from anyone else.

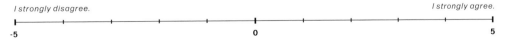

I strongly disagree.   *I strongly agree.*

-5   0   5

QUESTIONS CONTINUE ON NEXT PAGE ⟶

Discussion Questions (continued)

IF YOU HAVE CHILDREN...

13. Providing financially for my family is one of my most important responsibilities.

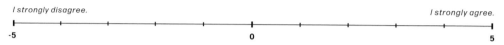

I strongly disagree.   *I strongly agree.*

-5   0   5

14. I want to give my children more than I had growing up.

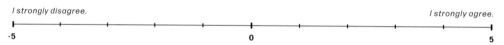

I strongly disagree.   *I strongly agree.*

-5   0   5

15. It's important that my children have the same things and opportunities as their peers.

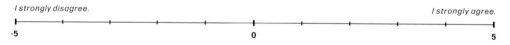

I strongly disagree.   *I strongly agree.*

-5   0   5

16. Children should be told the details of our family finances.

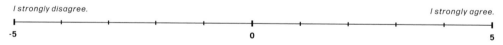

I strongly disagree.   *I strongly agree.*

-5   0   5

17. Giving my kids nice things is one way I show them I love them.

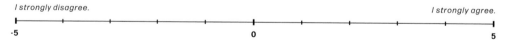

I strongly disagree.   *I strongly agree.*

-5   0   5

18. Once my children are old enough to earn their own money, they'll be expected to cover some of their expenses.

I strongly disagree.   *I strongly agree.*

-5   0   5

B) As a group, discuss these questions:

- Which statements did you strongly agree or strongly disagree with? What might have influenced your answers?

- Which statements (if any) made you feel conflicted?

3 | Andy said in the video that greed "is the assumption that it's all for my consumption." What's your reaction to this definition of greed?

4 | Has your financial situation ever impacted whether you were able to do something you felt called to do? Or do you know anyone else whose finances dictated their decisions?

For example: Your friend wanted to stay at home with her kids, but she had $50,000 in student loan debt, so she couldn't afford to leave her job.

BEFORE THE NEXT SESSION . . .

1 Follow the instructions on page 16 to take the Money Quiz.

2 Read more about your quiz result and find answers to common questions beginning on page 17.

TAKE THE MONEY QUIZ

Let's figure out what your relationship with money looks like today. The quiz will take about 10 minutes to complete.

Take the quiz digitally at

ifmoneytalked.com/quiz

Once you've completed the quiz, you can read more about your result and find answers to common questions beginning on page 17.

IF MONEY TALKED

If you aren't able to complete the quiz digitally, read the four descriptions beginning on page 18 and decide which one best captures your current relationship with money.

COMMON QUESTIONS AFTER TAKING THE QUIZ

- ## How was my result calculated?

  The general pattern of your answers is what's reflected in your final result. It is a high-level snapshot, which means your relationship with money may be very good in some ways and struggling in others. Your result merely describes your relationship with money *in general*. It does not capture every facet of your personal situation, so consider it just one way God may be challenging you to grow as it relates to your finances.

- ## What if I disagree with my result?

  That's okay. Money is a complicated, personal topic, and this one data point may not accurately reflect everything going on in your finances. (For example, couples divide financial responsibilities in many different ways, and each spouse's quiz result captures only part of the story.) As you move through the rest of this study, keep your result and your reaction to it in mind. You will not be asked to share, but see if you can figure out in what specific ways your quiz result might be inaccurate and in what ways it might be reflecting something you haven't noticed or questioned before.

- ## Why is my result different than my spouse's?

  You and your spouse may share the same financial accounts and have the same net worth, but you each have a unique relationship with your money that reflects experiences and attitudes that are likely different for each of you. And typically, the responsibility of handling joint finances is not equally shared. This is not a problem, but if you are more or less engaged than your spouse in money decisions, your relationship with money (and therefore your quiz result) is likely to be different than theirs.

- ## I have a lot of money, so why is this my result?

  This quiz aims to give you a snapshot of your relationship with money, not your net worth. It's possible to have plenty of financial margin and also have a view of money that may not align with God's. Personal finances are complicated, and your account balance and your attitude toward money are not necessarily linked. As you move through the rest of this study, consider how you might cultivate a perspective on money that's as healthy as your bottom line.

- ## Can my result change?

  Yes! Like any relationship, your relationship with money is not static. You may have happy, healthy seasons, and you may have times when your relationship with money is challenging. If you are discouraged by your result, there's good news: change can happen very quickly. Improvement requires only an attitude shift. And if you're satisfied with your result (high five!), know that the healthy perspective of money you have right now will take some effort to maintain. But as you likely already know, that effort will be well worth it.

Your relationship with money is ...
Living the Dream.

You and money have a healthy, happy relationship. Whether it's been smooth sailing for ages or you've worked your way here recently, you're enjoying real financial freedom. You have embraced your role as a manager of resources that ultimately belong to God, and your saving, spending, and giving plans reflect that. You responsibly save for your future without crossing the line into hoarding. You adjust your spending and your lifestyle to stay within your means. And you view generosity as a priority and a privilege. You think of money as a tool—not an entitlement—and you leverage it to love and serve others well.

What an admirable example you're setting. Bravo!

AS YOU MOVE THROUGH THE REST OF THIS STUDY, HERE ARE SOME QUESTIONS TO CONSIDER:

- **Are you "on your guard"?**

  Your relationship with money is not static. You'll have to continually reject the false assumption that every dollar coming to you is meant for you. What guardrails do you have in place to protect your perspective on money? Jesus' warning to be "on your guard" may be meant for you as urgently as anyone else.

- **Are you using money for its maximum impact?**

  You gauge the value of an investment on its potential return. Have you looked at your giving in the same way? Is it going toward things you feel uniquely called to address?

- **Who needs to see your example?**

  Your view of money is uncommon. But Jesus didn't want it to be. So, for whom could you model a healthy, happy relationship with money?

Your relationship with money is …
Going Steady.

You and money may have occasional up-and-down moments, but your relationship is on solid ground. You have long-term goals and are taking the short-term steps to achieve them. Generally, you spend and save wisely; when you don't, you get back on track quickly. You probably don't have much conflict with family or friends over finances. And you understand your responsibility to be generous (even if you sometimes stop short of putting that extra zero on a donation).

Your responsible money management deserves a high five!

AS YOU MOVE THROUGH THE REST OF THIS STUDY, HERE ARE SOME QUESTIONS TO CONSIDER:

- **Have you shifted into autopilot?**

  A comfortable relationship with money makes it easy to get complacent—to be satisfied spending some, saving some, and giving some away every once in a while. But that's often when a dangerous assumption takes root—one that may keep you from financial freedom in the long run.

- **Have you lost track of some goals—especially the ones related to being generous?**

  We all know what it's like to *feel* generous when confronted with a need that tugs at us. But generous feelings don't feed hungry kids or fund cancer research. What could you accomplish if you decided to put your money where your heart is?

- **Have you prioritized the right thing?**

  You're likely happy (at least most of the time) with your levels of spending and saving. But by focusing your attention on those, are you missing the forest for the trees?

Your relationship with money is … Well … It's Complicated.

Like an "on again, off again" relationship, you and money have had moments of easy calm and moments of messy conflict. Perhaps you and money are "on a break" thanks to a spouse who handles the money decisions. Your relationship didn't end on bad terms, but you and money don't talk directly anymore. If it's not joint finances that are complicating your relationship with money, it may just be that budgeting feels boring and hard, and what's the use anyway? You've tried sticking to a spending plan, but something always knocks you off course. You've saved when you could but haven't quite made it a habit—it's hard when there are bills (or debts) to pay. Whether you're calling the shots or counting on your spouse, you and money could use a relationship tune-up.

The specifics of your financial situation are complicated, so it's worth celebrating that you're willing to think (and hopefully talk) about this topic.

AS YOU MOVE THROUGH THE REST OF THIS STUDY, HERE ARE SOME QUESTIONS TO CONSIDER:

- **What are you justifying?**

  Are you letting yourself off the hook for a habit you know you should change? *I'm not a numbers person. I don't have time to figure it out. Everyone else does it this way.* These excuses may make life easier now, but not forever.

- **Is your heart in the right place?**

  It's easy to get overwhelmed by the mechanics of money—credit card terms, debt payment plans, balance transfers, etc. But aligning your view of money with God's view of money *first* will bring clarity to all the steps that follow.

- **What hangs in the balance for you?**

  Jesus said more about money than just about anything else. Why was it so important to him? Perhaps because of how important it could be to *you*.

Your relationship with money is ...
On the Rocks.

You and money have a struggling relationship that is likely causing you to feel stressed, anxious, or hopeless. Perhaps your unsteady financial situation traces back to a health crisis or family emergency; maybe you lost your job or were forced to take unpaid leave. Now, every month (perhaps every day in your toughest seasons), your finances control you. Money has ruined relationships, the stress has taken a toll on your health, and your financial situation has forced you into choices you didn't want to make. You may be stuck in a cycle of unhealthy, unwise spending. Or you may be taking saving to the extreme—measuring your security by how much money you have in the bank, even when that comes at a cost to your loved ones.

Money is a painful topic for you, so you deserve a big measure of credit for engaging in this study.

AS YOU MOVE THROUGH THE REST OF THIS STUDY, HERE ARE SOME QUESTIONS TO CONSIDER:

- **What's the truth ... *really?***

  Your view of money is likely a blend of messages you internalized in childhood, habits you picked up by watching others, and lessons you adopted or rebelled against. So, if you're looking to justify your current behavior, you have plenty of factors to choose from. But rather than making excuses, what's the truth behind your circumstances ... *really*?

- **Are you willing to entertain another way of thinking about money?**

  You may need to adjust some behaviors around spending and saving, and the surest way to do that is to first adjust your beliefs. Are you ready to do some head and heart work? It may be what finally turns things around for you financially.

- **What do you want your story to be?**

  There may be a choice, a circumstance, or even a season you'd like to change as it relates to your finances. A do-over may not be possible, but could that season become one piece of a story you'll one day be proud to tell?

THE CONSUMPTION ASSUMPTION

SESSION 2

Masters

or

Master's?

AS A GROUP, IN SESSION 2...

(1) Watch the Session 2 video. *(15 minutes)*

(2) Discuss the questions that begin on page 26.

ON YOUR OWN, BEFORE SESSION 3...

(1) Read pages 30–33.

(2) Start spying on your money. Use the method you chose during group discussion on page 29.

(3) If you manage money with someone else, read *Bridging the Gap: Tips for Couples* on pages 36–37.

THE MOMENT
YOU THINK
YOU OWN ME,
I ACTUALLY
OWN YOU.

—*Money*

▶ Most of us allow our income to drive our spending.

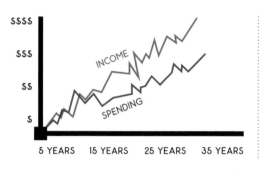
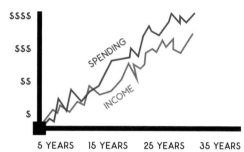

▶ When your spending exceeds your income, you become a slave.

▶ We know we are managers—not owners—of our money because one day we will leave it all behind.

AGAIN, IT WILL BE LIKE A MAN GOING ON A JOURNEY, WHO CALLED HIS SERVANTS AND ENTRUSTED HIS WEALTH TO THEM. TO ONE HE GAVE FIVE BAGS OF GOLD, TO ANOTHER TWO BAGS, AND TO ANOTHER ONE BAG, EACH ACCORDING TO HIS ABILITY. THEN HE WENT ON HIS JOURNEY... AFTER A LONG TIME THE MASTER OF THOSE SERVANTS RETURNED AND SETTLED ACCOUNTS WITH THEM.

—————— Matthew 25:14-15, 19

▶ When you manage someone else's money, you are responsible and accountable.

▶ The reason you should keep track of where your money is going is that it's not your money.

Discussion Questions

1 | Talk about a time you've seen someone experience consequences because of their spending (or saving).

2 | What's your first reaction to the idea that you are managing money that God has entrusted to you? Does that match the way you've thought about money before now?

3 | The challenge this week is to spy on your money.

A) Mark the box that describes you as it relates to knowing where your money is going *right now*.

I avoid thinking about it.	I'm mostly unaware of where it's going.	I know in general where it's going.	I know exactly where it's going.

B) As a group, discuss the following:

- If you're comfortable doing so, share and explain your answer.
- At other times in your life, would you have answered differently?

C) If your group includes couples, continue by discussing these questions:

- How do your answers compare with your spouse's answers?
- What do you like or dislike about that arrangement?

4 | As you're spying on your money this week, it may be helpful to ask: *Am I spending my money on the things that are most valuable to me . . . really?* The exercise below will help you think through what those things may be.

A) Take a few minutes on your own to write down which four things from the list below are most valuable to you in your current season of life. Then briefly describe why.

I would spend money on . . .	Because . . .
Example: Housecleaning/lawn service	*Time is my most precious commodity right now.*
1.	
2.	
3.	
4.	

Gym membership	**Pet(s)**	**Experiences** *(concerts, season tickets, theater)*
Travel	**Hobbies**	
Eating out/coffee out	**Gifts**	**Extras for your kids** *(travel sports, new clothes, technology)*
Date nights	**Home improvement** *(renovations, new decor)*	
Housecleaning/lawn service	**Self-care** *(hair and nail care, massages, anti-aging treatments)*	**Convenience services** *(meal/grocery delivery, laundry service)*
Vacation home/ second home		
Technology	**Luxury vehicle** *(car, motorcycle, boat, RV)*	**Paying off debt** *(mortgage, car loan, credit cards)*

QUESTIONS CONTINUE ON NEXT PAGE ⟶

B) As a group, discuss the following:

- What did you choose and why?

- Talk about a time when you prioritized (even grudgingly) what was valuable to someone else, even though it wasn't as important to you.

  For example: Your spouse spends money on a gym membership, which isn't a priority for you. Or family vacation is important to your mom, so you paid to go along.

C) Off the top of your head, write down a few things you've spent money on recently. Then consider whether those expenses align with the four things you identified as valuable to you right now.

I spent money on...	Is this one of the four things I value?
Example: Eating out for lunch twice	*No*

D) As a group, discuss where you may be spending money on things you don't *really* value. Do you have a choice in the matter?

5 | This week, you'll track your money to find out where you typically send it and spend it. Select the method you'll use to spy on your money.

☐   **Go digital.**
Use a digital money management tool to track all of your transactions. If you don't already use one, you can find a list of apps and software tools by visiting **ifmoneytalked.com/tools**.

☐   **Keep a paper trail.**
Save the receipt for every purchase you make. Store the receipts in an envelope or folder. Then, at the end of the week, record them on the *Tracking Your Spending* worksheet on pages 34-35.

☐   **Write it down right away.**
Carry a notebook (or keep a note on your phone) and record every expense right away.

☐   **Spend the same way.**
Use only one credit card or debit card all week. Then use the card's transaction history as the record of your expenses.

Note: If you share joint accounts with someone else, spy on your money together. Combine your expenditures and track them in one place.

BEFORE THE NEXT SESSION . . .

① Read pages 30–33.

② Start spying on your money using the method you chose at the end of group discussion.

③ If you manage money with someone else, read *Bridging the Gap: Tips for Couples* on pages 36–37.

Session Reading: *How to Apply Session 2*

LIVING THE DREAM

Your healthy relationship with money means you probably have a plan for your personal finances. You're investing, insuring, and maybe even getting help from other people to manage your money well.

That is so wise.
It's also so dangerous.

Here's why: Being in control of your finances makes it easy to develop the false impression that you control your finances. When you're the one earning your money, deciding what to do with it, and being thanked for giving some of it away, it's natural to believe the money is yours. The gravitational pull is toward *ownership*, not *stewardship*.

This is why you should really (yes, *really*) spy on your money this week. Tracking your spending—even when you have enough that you don't need to—is a habit that reminds you the money is not yours. It's a discipline not for your head, but for your heart.

MY THOUGHTS

....

....

....

....

....

....

GOING STEADY

If you loaned your friend a book and they misplaced it, you probably wouldn't be overly upset. But if you loaned them your car and they lost track of it? Well, that's another story. The larger the sum of money at stake, the more diligent we'd expect someone to be with what we entrusted to them.

You likely have enough margin in your finances that tracking every dollar you spend, invest, or save isn't a necessary habit from culture's perspective. But could that financial margin be the very thing that makes it necessary from God's perspective? You've been entrusted with more—more square footage, more cars, more clothes, more food, and more discretionary income—than most of the world. Do you feel the weight of that responsibility?

Tracking your spending may not be necessary, but it is in your best interest. It could relieve your hesitations about generosity because you might find out that things aren't as tight as they seem. Or it could appease your guilt by showing you how disciplined you actually are in your spending. Give it a try this week. You might be surprised at how helpful it really is.

MY THOUGHTS

....

....

....

....

....

....

IT'S COMPLICATED

The fastest way to learn a lesson is to experience immediate consequences: *Touch the hot stove, get burned, learn to check before you touch it next time.* Unfortunately, personal finances don't often work like that. You can spend several seasons of your life ignoring wisdom as it relates to your money, and you may not feel any immediate effect.

You could go months without logging in to your bank account, and the worst that may happen is you forget your password. Credit card companies will allow you to make minimum payments for the rest of your life. You'll go deeper in debt, but you won't get in trouble.

Money has a much longer feedback loop. The stress may not show up for years—until loan payments start, market conditions change, or your spouse can't handle money matters anymore.

Finances follow the law of the harvest: *sow now, reap later.* Tracking your spending is a way to sow now. Beginning—in an easy way, really—to get a handle on where your money is going may be a decision you look back on years from now and are glad you made.

MY THOUGHTS

....

....

....

....

....

....

ON THE ROCKS

When the bills come in, *other* people are dictating how you spend your money. The credit card company forces you to pay a certain amount every month. Next, the car dealership. After that, the mortgage company. When you owe someone else money, they own a piece of you—your time, your focus, your flexibility.

How freeing would it be to be able to decide what to do with the money God sends your way?

Financial freedom isn't an enormous sum of money; it's the ability to choose for yourself what to do with whatever sum of money you have—which means it may be much closer than you think.

In fact, spying on your money this week could reveal just how close financial freedom may be. As you track where your money is going, you'll see who currently owns pieces of you. Hopefully you'll see that, in many cases, you can decide otherwise. You can stop spending those dollars. You can cancel. You can hold off on the upgrade. Figuring out where your money is going may be the first step to financial freedom—and it may not be far away.

MY THOUGHTS

Tracking Your Spending

If you prefer to track your expenses with pen and paper, use this worksheet to record your transactions.

Date	Description	Amount
		$.
		$.
		$.
		$.
		$.
		$.
		$.
		$.
		$.
		$.
		$.
		$.
		$.
		$.
		$.
		$.

*For a printable copy of these pages, go to **ifmoneytalked.com/tools**.*

Date	Description	Amount
		$.
		$.
		$.
		$.
		$.
		$.
		$.
		$.
		$.
		$.
		$.
		$.
		$.
		$.
		$.
		$.

Bridging the Gap: Tips for Couples

WHAT IF YOU AND YOUR SPOUSE VALUE SPENDING MONEY ON DIFFERENT THINGS?

The next time you're about to spend money on something your spouse doesn't value as highly as you do, consider...

- **Pausing.**

  Being thoughtful in how you spend your shared money communicates honor to the other person. You may still decide to spend the money, but it's valuable just to stop and consider them first.

  For example: I'd love to buy tickets to that concert. That would be a lot of money to spend on something she wouldn't enjoy as much as I would, though.

- **Acknowledging it.**

  Unexpressed gratitude can feel like ingratitude or entitlement. So, make a point to thank them for supporting the expense. It can be as simple as a text message.

  For example: I know the tickets aren't a priority for you. Thanks for supporting something I love!

- **Reciprocating.**

  It's not productive or healthy to keep a financial scorecard in your relationship, but sometimes it's appropriate to balance the scales by intentionally prioritizing what they value.

  For example: Because we spent money on tickets last month, would you like to plan a night out with friends this month?

The next time your spouse is about to spend money on something you don't value as highly as they do, consider...

- ## Focusing on the *why*.
  Focusing on why the expense is important to them—on what value it brings or need it fills—helps you understand their perspective.

  For example: Even though I don't value the concert tickets, I do value the opportunity they'll give him to unwind and enjoy something he loves.

- ## Talking it over.
  Respectfully acknowledge the difference in your values. Sometimes their decision is based on a misunderstanding.

  For example: I do like that band. But I want to be honest that it's not my first choice for how we spend our extra time and money.

- ## Responding generously.
  View decisions like this as opportunities to show your spouse love and grace.

  For example: I might rather spend money on other things, but I love you and if it's important to you, it's important to me.

A Flipped Script

(1) Watch the Session 3 video. *(16 minutes)*

(2) Discuss the questions that begin on page 44.

(1) Read pages 50-53.

(2) Complete the *Give, Save, Live* exercise on pages 54-57. *(15 minutes)*

(3) Continue to spy on your money. And this week, start looking at where it's being sent and spent by working through the *Looking at the Line Items* exercise on page 59. *(30 minutes)*

MY DIRECTION REVEALS YOUR ULTIMATE AFFECTION.

—*Money*

▶ There are essentially five things you can do with money:

1. SPEND IT.
2. REPAY DEBT.
3. PAY TAXES.
4. SAVE IT.
5. GIVE IT.

▶ Most of us do those five things in that order (i.e., "me-first living with some leftover giving").

FOR WHERE YOUR TREASURE IS, THERE YOUR HEART WILL BE ALSO.

_____ *Matthew 6:21*

▶ What you spend your money on reveals what you care about most.

BUT SEEK FIRST HIS KINGDOM AND HIS RIGHTEOUSNESS,
AND ALL THESE THINGS WILL BE GIVEN TO YOU AS WELL.

_____ *Matthew 6:33*

▶ Jesus invites us to reprioritize.

1. GIVE FIRST.
2. SAVE SECOND.
3. LIVE ON THE REST.

▶ Pay attention to the tension. *Why am I resisting this?*

Discussion Questions

1 | Andy used a new car as an example of the principle that "what gets our money gets our attention." What's one example of something that *got your money* and consequently *got your attention*?

2 | In our culture, "me-first living with some leftover giving" is the typical way to handle money. How is that similar to or different from what was modeled for you growing up?

3 | In the video, Andy said, "There are essentially five things you can do with money."

▶ Spend it. *(Me)*

▶ Repay debt. *(Me)*

▶ Pay taxes. *(Me)*

▶ Save it. *(Me)*

▶ Give it. *(God and others)*

A) On your own, review your expenses from last month using the table and word bank on the following page.

 • Estimate which five expenses claimed the biggest chunks of your income last month and write them in the left column. (Use the options in the green box if you need help getting started.)

 • Then, in the right column, write down which of the "five things you can do with money" describes each expense. (You will likely have repeats.)

B) As a group, discuss whether it's realistic for one of your five biggest expenses to fit the *Give it (God and others)* category.

Food (groceries, eating out)

Utilities

Student loan payment(s)

Car loan payment(s)

Mortgage payment(s)

Health insurance premiums

Car insurance premiums

Phone, TV, and Internet

Tuition

Alimony/child support

Charitable giving (to a non-profit, church, school, etc.)

Long-term savings (retirement, college savings plans)

Investments

Car maintenance (gas, oil change, repairs)

Gym membership

Childcare

Home maintenance or renovation

Travel

Housecleaning/lawn service

Debt payments (on credit cards or back taxes)

Other: ....

Last Month's Top Expenses	Five Things You Can Do with Money
Example: Mortgage payment	*Repay debt. (Me)*
1.	
2.	
3.	
4.	
5.	

QUESTIONS CONTINUE ON NEXT PAGE ⟩

4 | Giving can either be reactive (after being asked) or proactive (before or without being asked). Read a few examples of each below.

Reactive	Proactive
• Contributing to a fundraiser after a natural disaster	• Donating to a nonprofit by running their 5K every year
• Chipping in when someone you know experiences a hardship	• Sponsoring a child or missionary overseas
• Giving after being asked in person on the street	• Giving regularly to your church

A) As a group, talk about which type of giving you lean toward and why.

B) Are you considering any changes? If so, what?

5 | Share the story of a powerful moment of generosity you've experienced (as the giver or receiver).

6 | When you think about giving away a percentage of your money (and doing it first), what tensions begin to surface? Check all that apply. If you feel comfortable doing so, share with the group.

☐ What if I need that money one day?

☐ It will take me longer to save (for a house, car, retirement, etc.).

☐ That money belongs to me. I worked hard for it.

☐ It will take me longer to pay off my debt.

☐ I might not have enough to give some away. I have bills to pay.

☐ I don't know what cause or organization I'd give to.

☐ Other members of my family won't be on board with this.

☐ Can I give later (e.g., after I get that promotion or pay off my student loan)?

☐ I already give more than most people.

☐ I won't be able to make ends meet.

☐ Other: ....

QUESTIONS CONTINUE ON NEXT PAGE

Discussion Questions (continued)

7 | Before Jesus said to "seek first his kingdom and his righteousness," he addressed the tension we might feel about flipping our financial priorities. Read his words in the passage below. Then, keeping in mind the tensions you just identified in question 6, share what part of the passage most resonates with you.

"THEREFORE I TELL YOU, DO NOT WORRY ABOUT YOUR LIFE, WHAT YOU WILL EAT OR DRINK; OR ABOUT YOUR BODY, WHAT YOU WILL WEAR. IS NOT LIFE MORE THAN FOOD, AND THE BODY MORE THAN CLOTHES? LOOK AT THE BIRDS OF THE AIR; THEY DO NOT SOW OR REAP OR STORE AWAY IN BARNS, AND YET YOUR HEAVENLY FATHER FEEDS THEM. ARE YOU NOT MUCH MORE VALUABLE THAN THEY? CAN ANY ONE OF YOU BY WORRYING ADD A SINGLE HOUR TO YOUR LIFE? AND WHY DO YOU WORRY ABOUT CLOTHES? SEE HOW THE FLOWERS OF THE FIELD GROW. THEY DO NOT LABOR OR SPIN. YET I TELL YOU THAT NOT EVEN SOLOMON IN ALL HIS SPLENDOR WAS DRESSED LIKE ONE OF THESE…BUT SEEK FIRST HIS KINGDOM AND HIS RIGHTEOUSNESS, AND ALL THESE THINGS WILL BE GIVEN TO YOU AS WELL. THEREFORE DO NOT WORRY ABOUT TOMORROW, FOR TOMORROW WILL WORRY ABOUT ITSELF. EACH DAY HAS ENOUGH TROUBLE OF ITS OWN."

—————————————— Matthew 6:25–29, 33–34

8 | In the video, Andy said, "The best way for your heavenly Father to take possession of your heart is to allow him to take possession of how you manage your money."

What (if anything) scares you about following God's advice about money?

How would you fill in this prayer?

> *God, I want you to have my heart. But, honestly, I'm scared that if I give you control of my money . . .*
>
> ☐ I'll have to give everything away (or do something I don't want to do).
>
> ☐ I won't get to have any fun.
>
> ☐ I'll fall behind everyone else.
>
> ☐ I won't be the one calling the shots anymore.
>
> ☐ ....
>
> *You already know this is how I'm feeling. Please help me work through my hesitation. Give me the courage to try it your way.*

BEFORE THE NEXT SESSION . . .

① Read pages 50-53.

② Complete the *Give, Save, Live* exercise on pages 54-57. *(15 minutes)*

③ Continue to spy on your money. This week, start looking at where it's being sent and spent by working through the *Looking at the Line Items* exercise on page 59. *(30 minutes)*

Session Reading: *How to Apply Session 3*

The merits of saving aren't up for debate. Appropriately preparing for your future is a way of loving others by sparing them undue burden. You know this, and your financial plan probably reflects that. Yet there's a tension to manage when it comes to saving—one you may not have considered before.

It's possible to save so much that your financial safety net supplants your need for God. You can achieve a level of financial independence that allows you to buy your way out of almost anything. You can hoard for a rainy day that never comes.

So, what's the right amount to save? Jesus didn't give us a percentage, but he gave us a mechanism for figuring it out ourselves. *He told us to give first.* When you experience the fun and satisfaction of channeling God's blessings to others, stockpiling them for yourself becomes less appealing. Giving is the safeguard against hoarding, which may be the most dangerous financial mistake you aren't protected from.

MY THOUGHTS

....

....

....

....

....

....

GOING STEADY

It can be hard to admit, but most of us feel more generous than we actually are. When it's a worthy cause, we contribute. When we're asked to give, we do. So, we conclude that we're generous. But if we're honest, much of our generosity is left up to chance, swayed by how often we're asked or how much we have left over.

That's *Giving 1.0*.

Are you ready for *Giving 2.0*?

Giving 2.0 is picking a percentage and proactively giving it away—without waiting to be asked or to be moved by a touching story. Rather than occasionally responding out of guilt that you have enough to spare, *Giving 2.0* acknowledges that God owns the money you're managing and it's not all meant for you. If you try it—if you take a premeditated approach to generosity—you'll probably be surprised at how much more money you give away. And you may be even more surprised by this: You will not miss it. Try it and see.

MY THOUGHTS

....

....

....

....

....

....

Session Reading: *How to Apply Session 3*

The financial script we each follow is basically the same. We make choices that can some-what alter our paths, but we eventually settle into more or less the same rhythm of *income in, expenses out*. So, if you handle money the typical way, you'll have plenty of company. Many people carry debt. Many people procrastinate about saving. Many people outsource money matters to their spouse. *Nothing's wrong with doing it this way. Everyone else does.*

Are you willing to try Jesus' way instead?

The truth is (and this is hard to admit), your answer reveals how much you trust God. The way you handle money right now probably feels fine. So doing it another way takes trust that it will be *better*.

Do you trust that giving money to others will be more satisfying than spending it on yourself? Do you trust that reengaging with your money might be a matter of faith more than finances? Jesus' way might not be easier, but you may find out it's better than the status quo.

MY THOUGHTS

....

....

....

....

....

....

ON THE ROCKS

We are bombarded daily with messages that tell us to be dissatisfied with our current circumstances—that it's time to upgrade, that we're falling behind, that everyone else already has one.

Discontentment is our default, which makes it nearly impossible to rationalize giving away money. *How can I afford to give away my money when I don't have enough to begin with?*

How about trying a smaller step first? Instead of being in an environment where you're constantly aware of what you *don't have*, place yourself in an environment where you become aware of how much you really *do have*. Tune out or log off, and then find a place where you're the one with plenty. You'll find out that discontentment disappears when you see what others need. And it will make flipping your financial priorities (which may feel impossible now) a step you're willing—even wanting—to take.

MY THOUGHTS

....

....

....

....

....

....

Give, Save, Live Exercise

The most systematic way to organize your finances around giving first, saving second, and living on the rest is to decide ahead of time what percentage of your income will go to each category.

Here are some steps that will help you discuss and ultimately make those decisions. Select which (if any) you'd like to try. Then when you're ready to commit to the percentages you'll give, save, and live on, fill them in on page 57.

GIVE

☐ **Pray about it.**

Invite God to guide this decision. Ask him to help you embrace the truth that you are a manager of his money.

Begin your prayer by reading 2 Corinthians 9:6–15, which captures what the apostle Paul wrote to a group of Christians about generosity.

☐ **Talk as a family.**

Discuss this decision with your spouse or another loved one. If you have kids, invite them into the discussion in an age-appropriate way.

 You can find tools to talk with your kids about all sorts of money issues at **ifmoneytalked.com/tools**.

☐ **Seek someone else's advice.**

Do you know anyone who is particularly generous or who organizes their finances around giving first? Ask for their counsel. Or talk with a financial planner, counselor, or mentor.

Write the names of one or two people you could talk with.

....

....

SAVE

☐ **Look to the future.**

What big expenses do you expect in the future? What are your long-term financial goals? The percentage you may want to save now depends on how much money you'll need and how soon you'll need it.

What big expenses do you anticipate in the next . . .

5 years?   **10 years?**   **20+ years?**

....

....

....

☐ **Consider matching.**

Some employers match contributions to your retirement account. If possible, maximize this benefit by saving at least the percentage of your salary that your employer will match.

My employer will match ....%.

I don't know the details of this benefit. I could ask ....

☐ **Aim for peace of mind.**

What will give you the peace of mind that you can handle an unexpected expense or circumstance? Use the filter of trying to be responsible and accountable with God's money—not trying to hoard for every possible occurrence.

Consider memorizing a verse or two from Jesus' comments about worry that are found in Matthew 6:25-34.

EXERCISE CONTINUES ON NEXT PAGE →

☐ **Include taxes, debt, and spending.**

After giving and saving, the amount you have left will go toward paying your taxes, repaying past debts, and covering your everyday living expenses. Do the percentages you're considering leave you with enough?

Let's do the math:

My annual income is $ ....:

If I give away ....% first, that leaves me with $ ....:

If I save ....% second, that leaves me with $ ....
to cover taxes, debt, and everyday expenses.

☐ **Keep your priorities flipped.**

It's tempting to shrink your giving and saving goals if you realize you might not have enough money left over to maintain your standard of living. How might your typical spending need to change in order to keep your priorities flipped to giving first, saving second, and living on the rest?

What's a current expense you're willing to consider (just consider) scaling back or giving up?

....

☐ **Spend according to your values.**

Last session's group discussion on page 27 helped you clarify a few of the things you value spending money on. If you can't afford everything you want, are you spending money *first* on the things you really value?

Turn back to page 27 and rewrite the four things you chose *in order of priority* below.

1. ....

2. ....

3. ....

4. ....

My Give, Save, Live Commitment

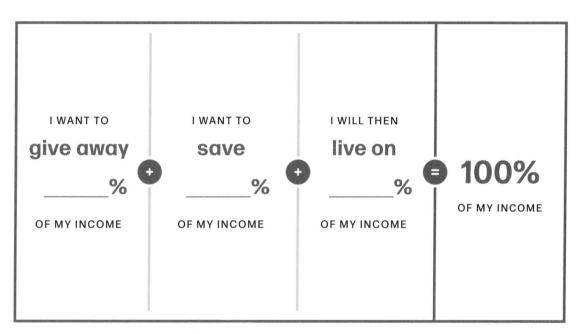

I WANT TO
give away
_____%
OF MY INCOME

+

I WANT TO
save
_____%
OF MY INCOME

+

I WILL THEN
live on
_____%
OF MY INCOME

=

100%
OF MY INCOME

Looking at the Line Items Exercise

Take 30 minutes to sit down and review the expenses you've tracked so far by working through the following steps.

Note: Most digital money management tools will automatically complete some of these steps. Hooray! Your work is partially done. But remember the warning from last session's video: "Knowing you can know is not the same as knowing." Take time to actually review your spending by category and work through steps 3 and 4 below.

1 | **Categorize every expense.**
Come up with your own categories (e.g., housing, transportation, entertainment, savings), and then group your expenses in order to get a high-level look at where your money has gone.

2 | **Break down the big expenses.**
Include monthly and/or annual expenses (e.g., rent or car insurance premiums) that may not have come up since you started tracking. Break down these big expenses into weekly or monthly portions.

3 | **Calculate your current percentages.**
Figure out the percentages of your income you're currently giving, saving, and living on. Are these numbers what you would have guessed? Which (if any) do you want to change?

4 | **Look for leaks.**
Flip back to page 27, where you identified four spending priorities. How well do the things you're actually spending money on match up with the things you wish you could spend money on? Look for places where your money may be "leaking"—where you're spending it on things you don't really value.

5 | If you're feeling like an overachiever: **Go way back.**
Bonus points if you dig up and look at your spending records for the past month or two. Reviewing a longer period of time gives you a more accurate sense of where your money has truly been going.

 Let's do this again sometime. Build a 30-minute review of recent expenses into your weekly or monthly routine. When would be the most convenient time to do this? Put it on your calendar now to start establishing this helpful habit.

Meaningful Money

AS A GROUP, IN SESSION 4...

(1) Watch the Session 4 video. *(12 minutes)*

(2) Discuss the questions that begin on page 66.

ON YOUR OWN, AFTER SESSION 4...

(1) Read pages 70-73 and identify a next step you'd like to take in your relationship with money.

(2) Visit **ifmoneytalked.com/next** for free bonus materials.

WHAT YOU CHOOSE TO DO WITH ME SPEAKS VOLUMES ABOUT WHO AND WHOSE YOU ARE.

—Money

"THE GROUND OF A CERTAIN RICH MAN YIELDED AN ABUNDANT HARVEST. HE THOUGHT TO HIMSELF, 'WHAT SHALL I DO? I HAVE NO PLACE TO STORE MY CROPS.'

"THEN HE SAID, 'THIS IS WHAT I'LL DO. I WILL TEAR DOWN MY BARNS AND BUILD BIGGER ONES, AND THERE I WILL STORE MY SURPLUS GRAIN. AND I'LL SAY TO MYSELF, "YOU HAVE PLENTY OF GRAIN LAID UP FOR MANY YEARS. TAKE LIFE EASY; EAT, DRINK AND BE MERRY."'

"BUT GOD SAID TO HIM, 'YOU FOOL! THIS VERY NIGHT YOUR LIFE WILL BE DEMANDED FROM YOU. THEN WHO WILL GET WHAT YOU HAVE PREPARED FOR YOURSELF?'

"THIS IS HOW IT WILL BE WITH WHOEVER STORES UP THINGS FOR THEMSELVES BUT IS NOT RICH TOWARD GOD."

—— Luke 12:16–21

▶ The mistake the rich man made was embracing the consumption assumption (i.e., he thought the extra was all for him).

▶ Money is a tool that can add meaning to your life.

▶ To what ends do you want your life to be a means?

- WHAT DO YOU WANT PEOPLE TO CELEBRATE ABOUT YOU WHEN YOU'RE GONE?

- WHAT DO YOU WANT PEOPLE TO LINE UP AND THANK YOU FOR IN THE END?

▶ If you'd like to change where your heart is, change where your money is going.

- GIVE FROM A GRATEFUL HEART.

- GIVE FROM A BROKEN HEART.

MEANINGFUL MONEY

Discussion Questions

1 | What's your tendency when it comes to extra stuff you no longer need?

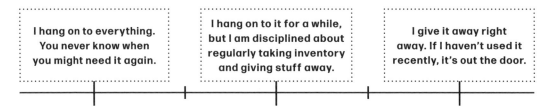

| I hang on to everything. You never know when you might need it again. | I hang on to it for a while, but I am disciplined about regularly taking inventory and giving stuff away. | I give it away right away. If I haven't used it recently, it's out the door. |

2 | In the video, Andy said that God views money as a tool we should use to make our lives meaningful. What do you think about that idea?

3 | Who have you seen be a good example of leveraging their money to make their life meaningful? (You may or may not know them personally.) Talk about what they did.

Can you think of anyone who has been a bad example—who had money but didn't use it in a meaningful way?

4 | "Where your treasure is, there your heart will be also" is a principle that works both ways. You can change where your heart is by changing where your money goes. Andy suggested doing that by giving from a grateful heart and giving from a broken heart.

A) On your own, spend a few minutes thinking about what that might look like for you.

What are you grateful for?

What organizations are currently serving your family well? What are you glad your kids are part of? What are you proud to be a member of? Who served your family in a time of crisis? Who made a difference in your life when you were younger?

Write down two organizations or institutions you're grateful for.

Example: My church

1. ....

2. ....

What breaks your heart?

What stories make you emotional? What injustice makes you angry? What problem do you wish you could magically solve? What cause have you always been passionate about? What have you experienced that you wish you could save anyone else from experiencing?

Write down two causes or needs that break your heart.

Example: Children in foster care

1. ....

2. ....

B) As a group, discuss these questions:

- What's something you're grateful for or brokenhearted about?

- If you're willing to share, what (if anything) has kept you from directing your money to the organizations and causes you just wrote down?

···················· QUESTIONS CONTINUE ON NEXT PAGE ····················⟶

5 | To figure out how to use your money to make your life meaningful, it may be helpful to think about one of the questions Andy offered in the video: *What do you want people to celebrate about you when you're gone?*

A) Let's put a twist on that question: *What do you want **your money** to celebrate about you when you're gone?* Write a sentence or two describing what you'd like your money to say. Here are a few options to get you started:

☐ You recognized that I belong to God and you were merely managing me for a while.

☐ You got your financial situation in good shape so you could say yes when you felt called to do things.

☐ You gave me for decades to an organization you were grateful for, even though they didn't ask.

☐ You responsibly managed me and tracked every expense even when you didn't need to.

☐ You put me where your (broken) heart was and gave generously.

☐ You flipped the script from "me-first living with some leftover giving" to giving first, saving second, and living on the rest.

....

....

....

....

....

....

B) As a group, discuss these questions:

- If you began viewing money as a tool for doing something meaningful with your life, what's the first change you would make?

- What (if any) hesitation do you have about making that change?

6 | We've looked at four pieces of advice money might give us *if money talked*. Which one resonated with you most? Where will you begin—what change (big or small) will you make in how you view or manage your money?

If money talked, it would say:	So, consider this next step:
"I can add meaning to your life, but I'm not the meaning of life."	Rethink the assumptions about money that may be hurting more than helping you.
"The moment you think you own me, I actually own you."	Figure out where the money you're managing for God is being sent and spent.
"My direction reveals your ultimate affection."	Make God and others your priority by giving first, saving second, and living on the rest.
"What you choose to do with me speaks volumes about who and whose you are."	Leverage your money to do something meaningful.

Congratulations! You've finished the study. Before you put this book on the shelf, though, let's figure out how you can help your takeaways stick. Turn the page to read a few next steps that will improve your relationship with money—no matter where it started four sessions ago.

Session Reading: *Your Next Steps*

Which of these next steps would help you apply the lesson(s) from this study that you most want to remember? Select one or two.

☐ **Answer Jesus' question.**

In the parable about the rich man who stored up his extra grain, Jesus posed a question worth applying to your financial plan: *Then who will get what you have prepared for yourself?* What's your long-term plan for the money you're making and saving right now?

☐ **Share your perspective.**

Most likely, you are very generous with your money. Can you be just as generous with your view of money? It may be uncomfortable to be seen being generous, but if others are able to see your example, they may be inspired to follow it.

☐ **Harness the right peer pressure.**

If the gravitational pull for all of us is toward the consumption assumption, who will help you remember that your extra is not yours?

☐ **Give your dollars purpose.**

You won't face a shortage of opportunities to give, save, or spend. But which ones match your personal passions? And if you manage money with a spouse, are their passions represented in your financial plans?

MY THOUGHTS

....

....

GOING STEADY

Which of these next steps would help you apply the lesson(s) from this study that you most want to remember? Select one or two.

☐ **Become a planned percentage giver.**

You can *intend* to be more generous for years—even decades. Don't let another season of life pass without turning your intention into action. Sort out the details and get started.

☐ **Invest in relationships.**

Money fills its proper role—as a tool—when you use it to enrich your relationships. Take your mom on the trip she's been dreaming of for years. Make memories at a concert with your son. You won't get a higher return on any other investment.

☐ **Adjust your standard of living.**

You'll know you're giving the right percentage first and saving the right percentage second when you occasionally have to adjust your financial plans to stay within the percentage you've decided to live on. Think of this as a financial guardrail protecting you from the consumption assumption.

☐ **Set your North Star.**

Whose example inspires you to give, save, or spend differently? Learn everything you can from or about them.

MY THOUGHTS

....

....

Session Reading: *Your Next Steps*

Which of these next steps would help you apply the lesson(s) from this study that you most want to remember? Select one or two.

☐ **Pay down your debt.**

There are many methods you can use to become debt-free. The one you choose isn't important. What's important is that you pick one and get started. Find a list of resources at **ifmoneytalked.com/next**.

☐ **Get involved.**

If your spouse handles the money in your family, take a step to become more engaged. It may help to ask yourself: *If they were suddenly unable to manage our finances, what would I need to know?*

☐ **Continue to track and tweak.**

Continue tracking where you spend your money. Then review expenses once a month and adjust future spending if any categories are out of line.

☐ **Invite someone else in.**

Many people (and couples) manage their money just like you. But seeing someone who does it differently—or someone who faced a challenge because they didn't— may convince you to try another way. Who has made different choices than you? Invite them to chat.

MY THOUGHTS

....

....

ON THE ROCKS

Which of these next steps would help you apply the lesson(s) from this study that you most want to remember? Select one or two.

☐ **Stop incurring new debt.**

You can't get out of debt if you keep going into debt. Be brave and cut up your credit cards to stop the outflow.

☐ **Continue to spy on your money.**

The habit of tracking your expenses (not even budgeting, just tracking) will make you more likely to spend wisely.

☐ **Fight discontentment.**

Spend time in a place that makes you aware of how much you have. And leave spaces (including digital ones) that trap you in comparison and discontentment.

☐ **Find a guide.**

Financial success stories almost always include a mentor, friend, or cheerleader that offered support. Find someone ready to help at **ifmoneytalked.com/next**.

MY THOUGHTS

....

....

....

....

If you're ready to take practical steps to improve your financial situation, we're ready for you.

You've finished the study, and perhaps your view of money has changed.

But are you overwhelmed by what to do next? Do you still feel stressed or stuck?

Visit ifmoneytalked.com/next

- Use the free bonus materials to take what was covered in this study a step further.

- Find recommended websites, apps, and books.

- Connect with someone who can answer questions and cheer you on.